CANADA

David Flint

SIMON & SCHUSTER
YOUNG BOOKS

ARCTIC
OCEAN

Arctic Circle

ALASKA

•Dawson
City

▲Mt Logan
6050m

CANADIAN   SHIELD

Hudson
Bay

•Churchill

C
A
N
A
D
A

Halifax•

ATLANTIC

O C E A N

0   400   800

Quebec
City•
Montreal▲
Ottawa• •St Lawrence Seaway
Toronto• ←Niagara
            Falls

Great Lakes

U

S

A

PRAIRIES

Edmonton•
Mt Robson
3954m▲ Mt Edith Cavell 3363m▲
Takakkaw   Lake Louise
Falls▲ Mt Victoria▲ •Calgary
         3464m

Rocky   Mountains

Fraser River

Vancouver•

PACIFIC OCEAN

Contents

Wheat is grown on the vast,
flat Prairies.

Many Canadians live in large cities
like Vancouver on the Pacific coast.

Ice-breakers are used to get through the frozen water of the Arctic Ocean

North country

Canada is the world's second largest country. It stretches from the Arctic Ocean in the north to the United States in the south. In the west, Canada meets the Pacific Ocean, and in the east, it meets the Atlantic. Canada is so wide from east to west, that when it is midday on the east coast it is only 7 o'clock in the morning on the west coast.

The weather in the north is bitterly cold and freezing for nine months every year. Summers are short and cool. The south has cold winters, but they only last about three months. Summers here are hot, and most people live in the south.

What is your weather like in winter, and in summer? How wide is your country from east to west, and from north to south?

Mountains and tundra

Ranges of the high Rocky Mountains
run down the western side of Canada.
The peaks are rugged and many, like
Mount Robson, are covered in permanent
snow and ice. The highest peak is Mount
Logan at 6,050 metres.

Across the centre of the country are the
flat plains of the Prairies. There are few
trees, here, because the ground is so dry.
In the east, the land rises again to a vast
area called the Canadian Shield where there
are forests, lakes, swamps, and bare rock.

In the north, the ground is frozen through
most of the year forming tundra.

Are there flat plains near you? What crops
are grown? What animals are reared there?

A moose feeds on mosses and plants in forest on the edge of the tundra in northern Canada. A fully grown moose can stand over 2.5 metres high.

The Angel glacier in the Jasper National Park tumbles down the mountainside from the ice field above.

The vast, treeless tundra of northern Canada. At the end of the short summer, the mosses turn bright red or orange.

Lakes, rivers and waterfalls

The Great Lakes, in south eastern Canada, are huge stretches of water. They are wide and deep and used by thousands of ships. The St Lawrence Seaway was built to connect the Great Lakes with the Atlantic Ocean. Now, ocean-going ships can sail far inland on the lakes to reach industrial cities like Toronto.

Many rivers flow north to Hudson Bay or the Arctic Ocean. Others, like the Fraser River, flow from the Rocky Mountains westward to the Pacific Ocean. In the east, the Niagara Falls on the Niagara River are world famous. The Canadian part of the falls is called the Horseshoe Falls, whilst the American Falls are in the United States.

Have you visited a waterfall? What was it like? Are there lakes near you? How big are they?

A grizzly bear catches salmon at a waterfall on the Fraser River in British Columbia.

At Takakkaw Falls in Alberta, the water drops 348 metres. Takakkaw means 'wow!' in the local Indian dialect.

Spirit Island on Maligne Lake, Jasper National Park in Alberta. Maligne Lake is just one of Canada's many lakes.

The town hall in Toronto, Ontario, has modern architecture in keeping with this forward looking city.

The Mounties with their famous red uniforms are the national police force. They have a reputation of always catching criminals.

Nearly a third of the people speak French, so road signs are in both French and English.

Inuit children dress in thick furs to protect them in the freezing winter weather.

People, provinces and territories

The first Canadians were the Indians and the Inuit who have lived in Canada for thousands of years. Later, much of Canada was a province of France, and then, in 1763, a British colony. Now, 45 per cent of the people have British ancestry, and 29 per cent French. The remaining 26 per cent are Inuit or Indian, or people from European countries like Germany or Italy.

Canada became an independent country in 1931. It has ten provinces and two territories. Each province has its own government and runs its own schools, police force and housing system. The parliament meets in Ottawa which is the capital city. Ottawa is in the province of Ontario where people speak both French and English.

Great riches

About a third of Canada is covered by forests. These are felled for timber, much of which is turned into wood pulp and used to make paper. The rest is used for furniture and veneers.

The best farmland is in the south. Here, Canada grows enough food to feed its people and has some left to export to other countries.

Valuable minerals like asbestos, gold, iron, lead, nickel, potash, zinc, silver and uranium are all found in Canada. Oil and natural gas from Alberta are piped to refineries in Ontario and the USA.

Are there forests near you? How big are they? What are the trees used for?

The Prairies of Alberta, Manitoba and Saskatchewan produce most of Canada's wheat. It is stored in huge elevators before being sent by rail to the towns.

About a third of Canada is covered by forest. Trees are felled and the logs floated down rivers to sawmills, as here in British Columbia.

Asbestos is mined in huge open pits like this one in Quebec. When mining is finished the holes are filled in.

Oil from Alberta is refined here in nearby Saskatchewan. Many things like petrol and paint are made from oil.

Life in Canada

Canada is a huge country with relatively few people, so there is plenty of open space. Canadians work hard and are well-paid and enjoy choosing how to spend their money. Shops open at 8.30–9.00 a.m. and may stay open until late. Some restaurants and food shops never close. French-speaking areas, like Quebec, have many open-air cafés and high quality restaurants.

Most families come together for the evening meal when they share their news. Older children do their homework after they have eaten. Television is popular—Canadians can receive many American stations.

What is your favourite television programme? How long do you spend watching television each day?

Corn eaten straight from the cob is popular with Canadians of all ages.

Winters can be very cold, and sometimes blizzards strike cities like Montreal.

Local artists display their work in the Rue du Trésor (Treasure Street) in Quebec.

Many Canadians take their holidays in the mountains, like here at the beautiful Moraine Lake in Alberta.

Public schools in Canada are free. This elementary school takes children aged 6-12 years.

Children board the school bus which collects them every day.

School days

Each province organises its own schools, so the system varies. In most places children start elementary school when they are about six years old. At twelve they go to junior high and at fourteen on to high school.

Public schools are free but private schools charge a fee every year. There are also some separate Roman Catholic schools. The school year starts in early September and continues until June.

In the far north some children go to live-in schools. They stay there during term-time because they live such a long way from a school.

What time does your school day start? What time does it end? How long are the summer holidays?

Because distances in Canada are so vast, many people travel by air.

The Inuit find motor tricycles a big help in crossing boggy tundra.

Electric-powered trolley buses are used in Vancouver to cut down on pollution from engine exhausts.

Railways are important because they carry most of Canada's heavy goods, like timber or iron ore.

Getting around

Most people travel to work or the shops by car. Petrol is quite cheap and cars are large and comfortable. However, for longer journeys jet planes are much quicker. Air travel has become as simple as catching a bus. Small planes land on remote lakes using floats in summer and skis in winter. They are a vital link with the outside world.

The St Lawrence Seaway joins the Great Lakes to the Atlantic Ocean. It is controlled jointly by Canada and the USA. The Seaway stretches 4,000 kilometres inland and ships carry wheat, coal and iron.

Are there railways near you? What do they carry? What is the most popular sort of car in your area? What do large trucks carry?

The huge, flat fields of the Prairies make it possible to use large, modern combine harvesters.

Huge salmon like these in British Columbia are a valuable catch.

The hot sunny summers in Quebec help tomatoes to ripen.

On land and sea

Fishing is important on the west coast in British Columbia. Here salmon are caught every year as they swim upstream to spawn. On the east coast, Newfoundland is the centre of the fishing industry and cod is the main fish. In the far north, the Inuit use modern power tools to drill holes through the ice before they can start fishing.

In Ontario, fruit and vegetables are grown, also tobacco and grapes. Further west the Okangana Valley is famous for its apples.

Have you been to the coast? What fish are caught there? What fish are caught inland?

City life

Eight out of ten Canadians live in cities.
Montreal is the second largest
French-speaking city in the world after
Paris. It is famous for its concerts and
theatres. Toronto, Canada's largest city,
is a major business centre. In Toronto,
the Canadian National Tower is the world's
largest self-supporting structure.

Quebec is the only North American city
which still has the original town walls.
Cities on the Prairies have wide streets
built on a grid pattern. Ottawa, the
Canadian capital, is a modern city with
tall buildings of glass and steel.

Are there tall buildings in the city near
you? What are the streets like? Is there
much open space or parkland?

The fantastic Château Frontenac in Quebec stands high above the St Lawrence river.

Jacques Cartier Square is in the old part of Montreal which was founded by the French in 1642.

Canada is governed from a majestic Parliament building in Ottawa.

Sport

In summer, baseball, tennis and golf are popular with many Canadians. Lacrosse is a national sport, and was adapted from an Indian game. Water sports such as white-water rafting, canoeing, water-skiing and scuba diving attract many people. At weekends, many Canadians go to cottages or camping grounds on lake shores. Others visit the National or Provincial Parks for hiking or mountain climbing.

In winter, ice skating, skiing and ice hockey are the most popular sports. Often people play ice hockey outside on natural ice.

What sports do you play? Which do you like best? Are there opportunities for water sports in your area?

When winter comes, rivers and lakes freeze solid. Ice hockey is a favourite winter sport.

In summer, many Canadians enjoy water sports like yachting here near Toronto.

Very like American football, Canadian football is played from July to November.

Famous landmarks

The Niagara Falls is one of the most popular visits for both Canadians and other visitors.

In autumn, the maple trees in the Ontario forests turn glorious shades of red and yellow, making a magnificent sight that is famous world wide.

The famous emerald waters of Lake Louise with ice-covered Mount Victoria in the background.

Beautiful Mount Edith Cavell is named after a First World War nurse. It is 3,363 metres high.

The Calgary stampede, which attracts many visitors, is a reminder that cattle ranching is still important today.

The CN Tower in Toronto is the tallest self-supporting tower in the world, at just over 553 m.

Facts and figures

Canada—the land and people

Population:	26,000,000
Area:	9,970,610 square km
Capital city:	Ottawa
Largest city:	Toronto
Population:	614,000
Languages:	French and English
Religion:	Christian—but others practised
Money:	Dollar ($) 1$ = about 43 p
Highest mountain:	Mount Logan 6,050 m

Main public holidays

New Year's Day	1 January
Good Friday	Friday before Easter
Victoria Day	Monday closest to 24 May
Dominion Day	1 July
Labour Day	first Monday in September
Thanksgiving Day	second Monday in October
Christmas Day	25 December

Special provincial holidays

St John the Baptist (Quebec)	24 June
Discovery Day (Yukon)	Friday nearest 17 March
St Patrick's Day	Monday nearest 17 March

Provinces and Territories

Territories	Capital cities
Yukon	Whitehorse
Northwest Territory	Yellowknife
Provinces	
British Columbia	Victoria
Alberta	Edmonton
Saskatchewan	Regina
Manitoba	Winnipeg
Ontario	Toronto
Quebec	Quebec City
Newfoundland	St John's
Nova Scotia	Halifax
Prince Edward Island	Charlottetown

Average temperature in Centigrade

city(province/territory)	January	June
Toronto (Ontario)	-4.4°C	21.8°C
Dawson City (Yukon)	-25°C	19°C
Churchill (Manitoba)	-20°C	15°C
Edmonton (Alberta)	-12°C	24°C
Montreal (Quebec)	-10°C	25°C
Halifax (Nova Scotia)	-4°C	19°C